The Poetry in Her Bones

A Collection of Poetry

Jacob Russell Dring

Since we met, whenever I think of poetry, I think of you. You are in every violin note and piano key.

You, loving you, and being loved by you is the greatest evidence of art anyone has ever thrust into my heart.

Peinture d'une Âme

I can taste the mist dancing from the sea
when my eyes lock with yours. And
when yours mirror mine, like planets
aligning, I can just about drown
happily.

Your sky smiles something gentle, a color unnamed but beautiful, eager not for a canvas but a current to carry it into other worlds.

I'd be smart to follow, but I'd have to be brave. And for you I feel everything, so there's nothing to worry.

Vegetation of inspiration, foliage of aspirations, now flourish in what were once boneyards. Knowing you has been a gift of life even when barrenness seemed too ruthless. You were and have always been my truest panacea. My effortless cure.

A garden thrives at your fingertips, music to
be heard and felt in ways that surpass sight.
Though what you've created and what you
will, in time, shall never be spared from the
senses. Not one. And the world is grateful.
Even if you don't hear it.

There is no better a word for the way wind
might dance with your hair or caress your face
and send little, dedicate sensations down your
spine and across your skin, than poetry.

I feel an exquisiteness to your existence, like a delicacy for those capable of perceiving it, and while I don't care to boast, I must admit some kind of pride for being given the honor of knowing you.

It's like talking to God, but then She talks back. And Her love is almost casual, not in its offering but its flow, like a light, aglow and pervasive. This is nothing shy of, nor exaggerated on, how I am pacified by sharing even a fraction of my life with you.

My nightmares are consoled by your
face, by the grace of your beauty, and
the touch of your palms, not to mention
the breath that wets your lips, even
when I am without hands, and sans a
voice, or the mouth that would carry it.

I adore your flesh but I am enrapt by
your incorporeal presence.

There is a kindness in your eyes incomparable to others. There are stanzas incapable of being written by anyone else. There is a glimpse of something I'd like to believe is proof that heaven or some version of it exists, whether in this life or the next. In your irises and the composition surrounding them is a sacred text that I'll always ache to read, but will never truly know the language, not as intimately as I wish.

I was not shown the genuine
truth of dreaming until I was
given a tour of your heart, and
the way it beats, especially how
it beat for me.

If I were to die with hope in my palm, rest assured that it was with peace, stitched there by the knowledge that you once loved me as the dry earth loves rain.

Seconds go by like days as I tiptoe into a floating trance, spiraling down the drain that is your soft blue stare. It is a sensory deprivation chamber that never fails to remind me how eagerly yet smoothly my pulse races for you, and just as easily, is lulled to rest. A heavy sleep, a pluvial dreamstate.

The color of your eyes, though inarguably vivid even when your skies seem gray, is irrelevant. They are not windows to the soul you possess, but for me, and anyone granted the opportunity to truly look into them, portals to the soul possessed by yours. A mirror for lovers. If even the unrequited, never the regretful.

A subtle tempest in your blood, I yield no surprise seeing it swarm like turquoise seagulls in your gaze, too. For you are a woman and it all makes sense, but there is little about you that strikes me with clarity. As much of a storm as you are, milady, you are both the eye of a hurricane and the surrounding maelstrom all at once. The truest definition of beauty, I'll not be convinced otherwise.

The melody of your laughter, whether supple or discordant, is an audible beacon cast across the gray ocean where I drift, lost but in that moment found, and the light in your voice will have surely saved me from whatever darkness I'd known.

There dwells a loveliness in your marrow
that cannot be explained away or written
off. There is nothing plain or elementary
about the way you tick. Your cogs are
oiled with a multipurpose ambrosia,
likely amalgamated with ground petals
plucked from an earth eager to give.

Whatever flower blooms in your bones,
it is not one easily ignored by passersby,
it is not effortlessly painted on a wall
and forgotten. It instead tickles the
nerves of those who look, and I mean
really look. As I always do, when I look
at you.

Get lost in you.

No amount of beauty or poetic narrative could subtract the fortitude and courage that is lain like mortar between the organs of your soul. Between the seams of your flesh. For you are a woman and you are a deity that can never be dismantled. Try as any man or monster might, you will always be immortal. To me. And to the world, even if they don't realize it. This is the adherence that binds my love.

Part 2

Savourez la Déesse

It is in your fuchsia temple that I surrender
my power. Let it be known that I still claw
at the heavens, reminiscing of the domain
you gave me, but betwixt your Hadean lips I
capitulate my sanity, and submit my
humanity to whatever divinity you pour
forth.

Damned be my soul dripping into your avid jaw. But the way you imbibe my unhallowed reverence is too hypnotizing to ignore. And far too splendid to bury without an epitaph.

Deep within your bosom is my salvation, as much as it is my condemnation. The sternum you press to my lust is a chthonic effigy itself, and together we mirror our aching selves, swelling like the tides you command in me, surging like the waves that crash in you. Lest you so simply breathe, and beckon from me a mortal contribution.

The protean currents that
disembogue from your
efflorescence are the nectarous
mediums which the gods use to
tantalize man.

Our holy art.

There is a natural, minimalistic, yet primally
extravagant, poetry in the way your body
mutely demands worship.

I dispossess the intrepidity of my valiance when I gaze into your eyes. And when they become like the sea in your marrow, wet and conductive, I am reduced to ruins intent on flooding yours.

Weaken me with your eyes, love. In this fragility I'll find my grandest strength.

To wake beside you is to experience rapture,
one millisecond suffices to witness paradise,
sunlight trickling through the glass, that starry
look on your face…yeah, baby, I guess I'm not
all atheist.

Your beauty is a kind that cannot be corrupted, but only complemented, by the distortions caused amidst toiled linen.

Art forms cast to the wind when you moan, when your body writhes not unlike the waves that you contain, and in due time, expel.

Too often do I throb undeservingly, every inch and fiber of my vessel yearning to find traction on your terrain, in your oceans, wanting not to just be held when you're able but to be drowned when you desire. And if you are so willing, so athirst, I shall not fail in my selfless worship.

My cross is suspended as you have hung
me like a figure on stained glass, painted on
my knees beneath ye, fervently swollen
with praise of your forbidden fruit and the
nectar to be split. Forgive my gluttony, but
I shall never not hunger for a taste, even if
it only be in written silence.

In the mausoleum of your least sturdy
tomb do I find myself buried, waiting
for it all to collapse upon me, be it
your carmine skies or your scarlet
abyss, but in the end I realize my
mistake, for your tremors are those of
strength and the bastion I've come to
inhabit will be the watery grave that
this old soul has sought for eons.

Your soul is food for thought. Your body…your skin…the rhythm of your heart when you contract and writhe…the rapid breaths spewing from your vibratory throat…or even the stillness of your form as you conduct the mundane, unbeknownst of the pulchritude you possess so idly…this all is food that nourishes me head to toe, even in places that have no mouth.

You stir the howls from a cauldron in my bones, the blood that rises like a beast in itself, with as little as the right kind of stare. Hundreds of yards. Thousands of miles. Millions of leagues. Billions of light-years. You deluge bridges and narrow distances until I am under your skin, pulling wires and tugging strings, not to manipulate but to play, to dance, to swim and smile and scream and growl as we were always meant to.

There isn't the smallest blemish or imperfection that doesn't warrant   salivation, on or within you.

    An anatomical servant of the senses, discarding the limits of humanity.

        You are art with a pulse, music with a flavor, and I love everything about you.